Dr. Jane Goodall @ 90

A Celebration and Reflection on Life and Career a beloved ethologist and conservationist (A Voice of Hope and word Of Wisdom)

Lauren R. Kelley

Table of Contents

Foreword

Jane Goodall, renowned for her groundbreaking work in animal rights and conservation, celebrated her 90th birthday with a powerful video message advocating for compassion towards animals. In the video, Goodall emphasizes the undeniable truth that animals possess personalities, minds, and emotions, urging viewers to recognize the depth of their experiences.

Joined by a host of famous friends including Ellen Burstyn, Alicia Silverstone, Mýa, and Sen. Cory Booker, Goodall's message resonates with empathy and urgency. Through a collective recitation of her words, the video highlights the emotional complexity of farm animals and the imperative to acknowledge their individuality and suffering.

Goodall's message extends beyond animal welfare to address the interconnectedness of all living beings and the urgent need for environmental stewardship. She warns against the destructive impact of human actions on the planet, emphasizing that by harming animals, we ultimately harm ourselves. The video serves as a poignant reminder of humanity's responsibility to protect and preserve the natural world.

Released through the Mercy for Animals organization and the Jane Goodall Institute (JGI), the video, titled "Voices of Hope — Words of Wisdom by Dr. Jane Goodall," encapsulates Goodall's lifelong dedication to advocating for a more compassionate and sustainable future. Leah Garcés, CEO and president of Mercy For Animals, lauds Goodall's transformative impact on generations and her unwavering commitment to positive change.

As Goodall reflects on her journey and milestone birthday, she emphasizes her desire to impart a message of unity and empathy for all beings. With a call to action for understanding, compassion, and love, Goodall underscores the pivotal role each individual plays in shaping a brighter future for the planet.

In celebrating her 90th birthday, Jane Goodall reaffirms her legacy as a tireless champion for animals, people, and the interconnected web of life that binds us all together.

Chapter 1: Early Beginnings

Born in London, England on April 3, 1934, Jane Goodall's upbringing was shaped by her middle-class British family. Her parents, Mortimer Herbert Morris-Goodall, an engineer, and Vanna Morris-Goodall, a novelist, fostered an environment that nurtured her fascination with animals from a young age. Goodall attended the Uplands private school, where she excelled academically, earning certificates in 1950 and 1952.

Despite societal expectations, Goodall's mother, Vanna, encouraged her daughter to pursue her dreams, instilling in her the values of perseverance and hard work. At just one year old, Goodall formed a deep connection with animals, symbolized by her cherished toy chimpanzee named Jubilee.

This early affinity for animals foreshadowed her future groundbreaking work in primatology.

Goodall's childhood was marked by moments of curiosity and determination, such as winning the trust of a pig and spending hours observing hens to learn about egg-laying. These experiences laid the foundation for her patient and meticulous approach to research later in life.

As a young adult, Goodall worked various jobs to finance her dream of traveling to Africa. At the age of twenty-three, she finally commenced her journey, arriving in Africa in 1957. It was there that she met renowned anthropologist Louis Leakey, who recognized her potential for studying primates.

Under Leakey's mentorship, Goodall began her historic study of chimpanzees in Gombe National Park. Leakey's discoveries of ancient human remains in Africa supported his belief in the continent as the cradle of humanity, inspiring Goodall's own research and shaping her understanding of human evolution.

Goodall's journey to Africa marked the beginning of her transformative career as a primatologist and conservationist. Her pioneering research on chimpanzees revolutionized our understanding of primate behavior and paved the way for advancements in conservation science. Through her lifelong dedication to studying and protecting wildlife, Goodall has left an indelible mark on the field of primatology and inspired generations to come.

Chapter 2: Research Pioneer

In the late 1950s, Jane Goodall visited South Kinangop, Kenya, at the invitation of a childhood friend, which ultimately led her to meet anthropologist Louis Leakey. Leakey recognized her potential and hired her as a secretary, inviting her to participate in anthropological digs and study the behavior of vervet monkeys on an island in Lake Victoria. Despite lacking formal scientific education, Leakey believed Goodall possessed the temperament for long-term fieldwork.

In July 1960, at the age of twenty-six, Goodall embarked on her pioneering study of chimpanzees in Gombe National Park, Africa. Armed with determination and a love for animals, she initially worked alone, gradually gaining the trust of the chimpanzees through patience and perseverance.

Goodall's groundbreaking research challenged prevailing beliefs about chimpanzee behavior, revealing their complex social structures and use of tools.

In 1962, Leakey facilitated Goodall's pursuit of a doctorate degree at Cambridge University, lending scientific credibility to her discoveries. By 1964, the Gombe Stream Research Center had become a hub for scientists and graduate students eager to study chimpanzees. Goodall's work gained widespread attention through National Geographic articles and television specials.

In 1964, Goodall married wildlife photographer Hugo Van Lawick, who documented her research. The 1970s brought new challenges, including violent conflicts and infanticide among the chimpanzees, prompting Goodall to revise her understanding of their behavior. Despite risks, she continued her work with the help of local researchers.

Goodall's focus later shifted to captive chimpanzees and conservation efforts. She advocated for improved treatment of animals in laboratories and zoos, co-founding the Committee for the Conservation and Care of Chimpanzees in 1986. Additionally, she authored children's books promoting kindness towards animals.

Throughout her career, Goodall's passion for animals and dedication to conservation have left an enduring legacy, inspiring countless individuals to protect wildlife and their habitats. Her work serves as a testament to the power of perseverance and compassion in creating positive change for the planet and its inhabitants.

Chapter 3: Advocate for Change

Transition to activism

At the Young Women's Veterinary Association International Conference on Sustainable Veterinary Practice, the animal calls echoed so vividly that one might have mistaken the room for a jungle, resonating with the unmistakable sounds of chimpanzees.

"This is me, this is Jane, in chimpanzee language," remarked primatologist Dr. Jane Goodall.

Hailed as the world's foremost authority on chimpanzees, Dr. Goodall, founder of the Jane Goodall Institute and UN Messenger of Peace, boasts a remarkable career adorned with accolades, including England's highest honor, Dame of the British Empire, conferred upon her in 2004.

Her tireless advocacy for humanitarian and animal rights causes has earned her widespread recognition.

Reflecting on her journey, Goodall recounted her unwavering passion for animals since childhood, harboring dreams of living among wild creatures in Africa and documenting their lives. Despite facing skepticism and societal barriers, her determination remained unshakable.

Under the guidance of renowned paleontologist and anthropologist Dr. Louis Leakey, Goodall embarked on groundbreaking research in 1960, delving into the behavior of chimpanzees at the Gombe Stream Chimpanzee Reserve in Tanzania—a venture unparalleled at the time.

Her groundbreaking observations, including chimpanzees using tools to extract termites from mounds, shattered conventional beliefs about animal intelligence, compelling a reevaluation of humanity's relationship with the animal kingdom.

Venturing into academia, Goodall pursued a Ph.D. at Cambridge University, only to encounter resistance from the scientific community, which dismissed her findings on animal sentience as unconventional. Despite the opposition, her convictions remained steadfast.

In 1986, a pivotal conference opened Goodall's eyes to the widespread habitat destruction and mistreatment of chimpanzees worldwide, igniting her transformation from scientist to activist.

Addressing contemporary environmental challenges, Goodall highlighted the detrimental impact of industrial farming on climate change, underscoring the urgent need for sustainable practices to mitigate ecological harm.

Despite the grim realities, Goodall remains optimistic, advocating for greater compassion and understanding toward animals as the key to addressing global challenges.

Nearly six decades since her groundbreaking research in Tanzania, Dr. Jane Goodall's legacy endures, challenging humanity to reconsider its relationship with the natural world. Embracing her role as an activist, she continues to champion conservation efforts and environmental education, leaving an indelible mark on both science and society.

Creation of the Jane Goodall Institute

The year 1977 marked a significant milestone in Dr. Jane Goodall's journey of environmental advocacy and conservation as she established the Jane Goodall Institute (JGI). This organization has become a beacon of hope, leading the charge for conservation efforts that resonate with people of all ages and backgrounds. At its core, the JGI is dedicated to empowering youth through various programs centered on conservation, reflecting Dr. Goodall's belief in the power of the next generation to effect positive change.

One noteworthy initiative spearheaded by the JGI is the Cycle My Cell campaign, which exemplifies Dr. Goodall's remarkable ability to inspire action. This campaign focuses on collecting old cell phones to reduce the need for mining precious metals in areas inhabited by great apes, thus mitigating environmental harm and preserving vital habitats.

The overarching vision of the Jane Goodall Institute is to cultivate a global movement of conservation that emphasizes the interconnectedness of all living beings and their habitats. Building on Dr. Goodall's legacy, the JGI instills hope through tangible actions, encouraging individuals worldwide to take responsibility for the well-being of our planet.

From restoring chimpanzee habitats to promoting women's health initiatives in local communities, the Jane Goodall Institute is committed to making a lasting impact on both people and the environment. Through its Roots & Shoots youth groups operating in nearly 100 countries, the JGI fosters a sense of stewardship and environmental responsibility among young people, empowering them to become catalysts for positive change.

Central to the JGI's approach is the integration of conservation science, leveraging advanced technologies and scientific methodologies to inform local communities and guide their conservation efforts. By equipping communities with the necessary tools and knowledge, the JGI enables them to develop and implement effective conservation action plans tailored to their specific needs and circumstances.

In essence, the Jane Goodall Institute continues to uphold Dr. Goodall's legacy of compassion, activism, and environmental stewardship, embodying her belief that each individual has the power to make a meaningful difference in the world. Through collaborative efforts and a steadfast commitment to conservation, the JGI remains at the forefront of the global movement to protect and preserve our planet for future generations.

Expansion of conservation efforts

Many are familiar with the remarkable story of Jane Goodall, whose groundbreaking research in Gombe transformed our understanding of chimpanzees and their intricate social dynamics. Yet, alongside her pioneering scientific endeavors, Jane embarked on another revolutionary journey – one focused on protecting these remarkable creatures and their habitats. The Jane Goodall Institute (JGI) was born out of this vision, and now, it's taking a monumental leap forward with the launch of a brand-new strategy.

This innovative strategy represents a bold step toward realizing Jane's vision for a more harmonious world, bridging the gap between conservation, community welfare, and youth empowerment. By honing in on what works best to safeguard great apes, enhance human well-being, preserve habitats, and nurture the next generation of changemakers through initiatives like the Roots & Shoots youth program, JGI is charting a course for a brighter future.

Central to this strategy is the unwavering commitment to Jane's mission – a mission rooted in the understanding that everything in our world is interconnected. For over six decades, Jane and JGI's research in Gombe have deepened our comprehension of chimpanzees and wildlife, laying the foundation for effective conservation efforts. With this new strategy, JGI aims to build upon this legacy by expanding its reach and impact, both in protecting apes and empowering communities.

At the heart of JGI's goals lies a dual focus: ensuring the conservation and welfare of chimpanzees and inspiring global citizens to make compassionate, sustainable choices. These goals are intertwined, as great apes, particularly chimpanzees, serve as a poignant reminder of our shared humanity and the urgent need for collective action to protect our planet.

To achieve these ambitious goals, JGI is leveraging its unique strengths and expertise across various fronts. From community-centered conservation initiatives like Tacare to groundbreaking research in Gombe and efforts to enhance chimpanzee welfare through sanctuaries, JGI is at the forefront of conservation innovation.

Furthermore, JGI's Roots & Shoots program stands as a beacon of hope, empowering youth worldwide to become agents of positive change through education and advocacy. By harnessing Jane's influence and legacy, JGI aims to inspire compassion-driven action and foster a global movement dedicated to biodiversity conservation and sustainable living.

This strategy isn't just a vision – it's a call to action. Through policy advocacy, scientific innovation, community engagement, and organizational growth, JGI is poised to tackle the pressing challenges facing our planet with renewed vigor and determination. By addressing these issues holistically and with unwavering optimism, JGI is turning Jane's vision into a reality, one step at a time.

Chapter 4: Global Impact

International recognition and awards

Dr. Jane Goodall's remarkable contributions to primatology and conservation have earned her widespread acclaim and numerous prestigious awards. Here are some highlights of her illustrious career:

1. **Templeton Prize (2021)**: In 2021, Dr. Goodall was honored with the Templeton Prize, marking a pinnacle in her six-decade-long career. This esteemed award recognizes her unparalleled insights into chimpanzee behavior and her relentless advocacy for wildlife conservation through initiatives like the Jane Goodall Institute and Roots & Shoots program.

2. **United Nations Messenger of Peace (2002)**: Acknowledging her dedication to promoting peace and environmental stewardship, Dr. Goodall was appointed as a United Nations Messenger of Peace in 2002, amplifying her global influence and humanitarian efforts.

3. **Lifetime Achievement Awards and Hall of Fame Inductions**:

- *Hubbard Medal (1995)*: Awarded in recognition of her groundbreaking scientific contributions and exploratory endeavors.
- *Tyler Prize for Environmental Achievement (1997)*: Honored for her tireless advocacy and leadership in environmental conservation.
- *National Jewish Sports Hall of Fame (2011)*: Inducted for her exceptional achievements and contributions to society.

- *International Marathon Swimming Hall of Fame (2014)*: Recognized for her remarkable accomplishments, transcending boundaries beyond her field of expertise.

Throughout her illustrious career, Dr. Goodall has received a plethora of prestigious honors and awards, including the Gold Medal of Conservation from the San Diego Zoological Society (1974), the J. Paul Getty Wildlife Conservation Prize (1984), the Schweitzer Medal of the Animal Welfare Institute (1987), the National Geographic Society Centennial Award (1988), and the Kyoto Prize in Basic Sciences (1990).

Additionally, she was bestowed with the title of Dame of the British Empire by Queen Elizabeth II in 2003, further cementing her legacy as a pioneering figure in the realm of conservation and humanitarianism.

Key initiatives and campaigns

Dr. Jane Goodall, an esteemed primatologist and environmental advocate, has dedicated her life's work to wildlife conservation and fostering environmental consciousness. Here are some of the pivotal initiatives and campaigns associated with her remarkable contributions:

1. **The Jane Goodall Institute (JGI)**
Established by Dr. Jane Goodall in 1977, the JGI is a globally renowned conservation organization committed to safeguarding chimpanzees, preserving natural habitats, and instilling a sense of environmental stewardship in communities worldwide.
JGI adopts a comprehensive approach that prioritizes the involvement of local communities in conservation efforts, thereby fostering sustainable

coexistence between people, wildlife, and their habitats.

2. Chimpanzee Conservation

Dr. Goodall's seminal research conducted in Gombe Stream National Park, Tanzania, revolutionized our understanding of chimpanzee behavior and social dynamics.
JGI's tireless efforts are geared towards preventing the extinction of chimpanzees. Alarmingly, the wild chimpanzee population has plummeted from approximately 1 million in 1900 to as few as 340,000 today.

3. Hope and Impact

Dr. Goodall's unwavering dedication instills hope for a brighter future. Through initiatives focused on chimpanzee protection, environmental conservation, and sustainable practices, she leaves a lasting impact on communities worldwide.

JGI's initiatives emphasize sustainability, ethical partnerships, and community-driven conservation efforts.

4. **Where in the World is Jane?**

Despite her global influence, Dr. Goodall remains actively engaged in educational endeavors, awareness-raising initiatives, and advocacy campaigns.

Stay updated on Dr. Goodall's upcoming activities and engagements, and join her in the collective pursuit of positive change for our planet.

As Dr. Goodall aptly reminds us, "Every individual matters. Every individual has a role to play. Every person makes a difference. Let us all join in responding to her call to action and working toward a more sustainable and harmonious connection with our natural environment.

Influence on policy-making and education

Dr. Jane Goodall, renowned for her tireless advocacy and profound wisdom, often reminds us that "the greatest danger to our future is apathy." She emphasizes that securing a sustainable future for all beings and our planet starts with understanding and education. Reflecting on her own childhood curiosity, such as her quest to unravel the mystery of how chickens laid their eggs, Dr. Goodall underscores the pivotal role of educators in nurturing a deep appreciation for the natural world.

Despite her demanding schedule, traveling over 300 days a year to share her insights worldwide, Dr. Goodall remains dedicated to her role as an educator. She encourages individuals to reflect on their daily choices, including consumption habits, diet, and clothing preferences, emphasizing how even small actions can make a significant impact. As a vegetarian herself, she illustrates how personal choices can align with environmental conservation goals. Dr. Goodall also places great hope in the next generation, advocating for equipping them with the knowledge and resources to tackle global challenges effectively. She underscores the power of collaboration, asserting that when intellect and compassion unite, humanity can realize its full potential.

Goodall's academic achievements are exemplary, culminating in a Ph.D. in ethology from Cambridge University in 1965. Remarkably, she became only the eighth individual in the university's history permitted to pursue a Ph.D. without a prior baccalaureate degree. She subsequently held a visiting professorship in psychiatry at Stanford University from 1970 to 1975 and was appointed an honorary visiting professor of zoology at the University of Dar es Salaam in Tanzania in 1973.

In response to attending a pivotal conference in 1986 focused on the ethical treatment of chimpanzees, Dr. Goodall redirected her efforts toward public education on the endangered habitats of wild chimpanzees and the ethical considerations surrounding chimpanzee research. Advocating for nature-friendly tourism initiatives in African nations, she collaborates with businesses and local governments to promote ecological responsibility and sustainable practices.

While acknowledging the complexities of animal research, Dr. Goodall advocates for the exploration of alternatives and urges for greater compassion in scientific practices. She condemns extremist approaches on both sides of the issue, emphasizing the need for constructive dialogue and ethical treatment of animals in research endeavors.

Dr. Goodall asserts that educating young scientists about compassionate practices is imperative, challenging prevailing norms that perpetuate animal suffering in the name of scientific progress. As she eloquently states, "By and large, students are taught that it is ethically acceptable to perpetrate, in the name of science, what, from the point of view of animals, would certainly qualify as torture."

Chapter 5: Personal Reflections

Marriages and Son

In 1962, Jane Goodall's life took a romantic turn when Baron Hugo van Lawick, a Dutch wildlife photographer and filmmaker, was assigned by the National Geographic Society to film her work in Africa. Their professional collaboration blossomed into love, and they married on March 28, 1964. Their European honeymoon marked a rare departure for Goodall from her beloved Gombe Stream. Their son, Hugo Eric Louis, affectionately known as "Grub," was born in 1967.

Following her divorce from van Lawick in 1974, Goodall married Derek Bryceson, a prominent figure in Tanzania's parliament and national parks administration. Sadly, Bryceson passed away from cancer in 1980.

Philosophically, Goodall reflects on humanity's perplexing propensity to harm its own habitat despite its intellectual capabilities. However, she finds hope in the passion of youth, the resilience of nature, and the enduring human spirit.

As a prominent conservationist and UN Messenger of Peace, Goodall continues to advocate for responsible living and combating climate change, which she deems as the paramount threat facing humanity.

On her 83rd birthday, April 3, 2017, Goodall shared her insights during the Commonwealth Club of California's "Climate One" series, hosted by Greg Dalton. Joining her was Jeff Horowitz, founder of Avoided Deforestation Partners and co-producer of National Geographic's "Years of Living Dangerously," who aimed to push Goodall beyond her comfort zone to engage with global leaders in effecting substantial change.

Movies and Documentary

The groundbreaking documentary "Miss Goodall and the Wild Chimpanzees," which premiered on American television on December 22, 1965, introduced the general public to Jane Goodall's pioneering work. Filmed by her first husband and narrated by Orson Welles, the documentary depicted the determined young Englishwoman observing chimpanzees in their natural habitat with patience and dedication.

This captivating portrayal of Goodall's interactions with the chimps quickly became a staple of American and British public television, challenging scientists to reconsider the traditional distinctions between humans and other primates.

In 2017, previously unreleased footage from the "Miss Goodall" filming was compiled for the documentary "Jane," which featured recent interviews with the renowned activist. This film provided a more comprehensive narrative of Goodall's experiences with the chimpanzees, offering viewers deeper insight into her remarkable journey and lifelong dedication to wildlife conservation.

Jane Goodall's Books and Controversies

Jane Goodall's extensive fieldwork yielded a wealth of publications, ranging from scientific articles to popular books. Her seminal work, "In the Shadow of Man," published in 1971, provided a captivating field study of chimpanzees that appealed to both scientists and the general public. While praised for its vivid portrayal of chimp behavior, some critics raised concerns about Goodall's tendency to anthropomorphize the animals.

In her 1990 book, "Through a Window," Goodall delved into the ethical implications of keeping chimpanzees in captivity, highlighting the moral dilemmas surrounding their use in various human activities, including entertainment, research, and as pets. She emphasized the need for greater consideration of the suffering inflicted upon animals in these contexts.

Goodall's commitment to promoting a more humane view of wildlife extended to her children's book, "The Chimpanzee Family Book," published in 1989. This book, which received the UNICEF/UNESCO Children's Book of the Year Award, aimed to instill empathy and understanding for animals in young readers.

However, Goodall faced controversy with her book "Seeds of Hope: Wisdom and Wonder from the Plants," co-authored with Gail Hudson, in 2013. Accusations of plagiarism arose when it was discovered that Goodall had incorporated sections from Wikipedia and other sources without proper attribution. The book's release was delayed for revisions to address these issues, and Goodall issued a statement expressing remorse for the oversight. "Seeds of Hope" was eventually reissued in 2014.

QUOTES

1. "For hundreds of thousands of years, chimps have lived in their forest, never overpopulating or ruining it. In terms of environmental stewardship, I believe they have outperformed us.

2. "The greatest danger to our future is apathy."

3. "The more we learn of the true nature of nonhuman animals ... the more ethical concerns are raised regarding their use in the service of man."

4. "By and large, students are taught that it is ethically acceptable to perpetrate, in the name of science, what, from the point-of-view of animals, would certainly qualify as torture."

5. "One of my earliest memories is of hiding in a cramped, stuffy henhouse to watch a hen lay an egg. I emerged after almost five hours. The entire household had evidently been looking for me for hours, and my mother had even contacted the police to declare me missing."

6. "When young people are informed and empowered, and they understand that what they do genuinely matters, they can change the world. "They are already changing it."

7. "When I initially started, I assumed the chimps were gentler than we are. However, time has shown that they are not. "They can be just as bad."

8. "To achieve global peace, we must not only stop fighting each other, but also stop destroying the natural world."

9. "[Chimps] have an evil side, just like ourselves. We have fewer excuses because we can deliberate, and I believe only humans are capable of genuine premeditated evil."

10. "If we are the most intellectual creature that ever walked on the planet, why are we destroying that planet?"

11. "My future seems ludicrous. I just crouch here, chimp-like, on my rocks, plucking out prickles and thorns, and giggle at the thought of this mysterious 'Miss Goodall' who is supposed to be performing scientific study elsewhere."

Chapter 6: Collaborative Efforts

Partnerships with celebrities and NGOs

Dr. Jane Goodall's impactful work has been further amplified through collaborations with various celebrities, organizations, and initiatives:

1. **"Conversations With Jane" Series**: Dr. Goodall engaged in intimate one-on-one conversations with leading Hollywood actresses-turned-activists, including Alicia Silverstone, Ashley Judd, Sophia Bush, and Nikki Reed. These discussions covered topics such as animal rights activism, nature's resilience, compassionate storytelling, and the power of hope. Dr. Goodall emphasized her work with Roots & Shoots, empowering youth worldwide to take action on critical issues.

2. **NASA Collaboration**: Partnering with NASA, Dr. Goodall addressed the impact of deforestation on chimpanzees and local communities in Western Africa. Utilizing satellite imagery from the Landsat series, she provided villagers with information on reducing harmful activities and preserving their environment.

3. **Brilliant Earth Partnership**: Dr. Goodall joined forces with Brilliant Earth, a company dedicated to sustainability and social responsibility. This groundbreaking partnership unites two female pioneers—Dr. Goodall and Beth Gerstein, Co-Founder and CEO of Brilliant Earth.

4. **60 Years of Groundbreaking Research**: Reflecting on her six decades of groundbreaking research, Dr. Goodall shares her wisdom and insights in various interviews and conversations,

continuing to inspire positive change worldwide.

Dr. Jane Goodall's tireless dedication and collaborative efforts serve to amplify her impact and inspire positive change across the globe.

Engagement with youth

Dr. Jane Goodall, the acclaimed scientist whose pioneering work in Gombe National Park shaped our understanding of apes, believes that the world is at a crucial juncture in how it perceives the critical relationship between nature and humanity.

For over three decades, Dr. Goodall's Roots & Shoots environmental education program has empowered children to enact positive change for people, animals, and the environment. The program, launched in 1991, has instilled values of conservation and activism in young minds, preparing them to become leaders in environmental stewardship.

Reflecting on the impact of her program, Dr. Goodall emphasizes the transformative power of youth engagement in conservation efforts. She believes that when young people are inspired and empowered to take action, they can make a significant difference in addressing global challenges such as climate change, biodiversity loss, and poverty.

While progress has been made in addressing biodiversity challenges, including the implementation of new policies and strategies to combat wildlife trafficking, Dr. Goodall highlights the ongoing threats to wildlife and human health. The illegal wildlife trade, fueled by social media and habitat destruction, poses significant risks, as evidenced by the COVID-19 pandemic's origins in a wildlife market in China.

Dr. Goodall commends conservation initiatives such as the recovery of the Arabian oryx from extinction, citing the UAE's significant role in these efforts. With the UN climate summit approaching, Dr. Goodall sees an opportunity for global leaders, including those in the UAE, to prioritize climate action and biodiversity conservation.

At 90 years old, Dr. Goodall remains steadfast in her commitment to environmental advocacy, continuing to travel the world to raise awareness about climate change and wildlife protection. She hopes to be remembered for her contributions to the Roots & Shoots program, which has empowered countless individuals to respect and protect the natural world.

Despite the challenges ahead, Dr. Goodall finds hope in the resilience of nature and the indomitable human spirit.

She believes that by working together and refusing to give up, people from all walks of life can overcome seemingly insurmountable obstacles and create a better future for generations to come.

Harnessing media and technology

Dr. Jane Goodall's connection to the world of information and communication technologies (ICTs) extends beyond her groundbreaking work in primatology. In collaboration with the tree-planting search engine Ecosia, Dr. Goodall has been involved in an innovative project to create 'forest corridors' in Uganda.

This initiative harnesses technology to address the pressing issue of habitat fragmentation, which threatens the survival of endangered species such as chimpanzees. By planting trees to establish corridors between forest patches, Dr. Goodall and Ecosia aim to facilitate the movement of animals and the exchange of genetic material, thereby promoting biodiversity and conservation efforts.

Key elements of this project include using a mobile phone app to monitor forest disturbances and maintain a database of tree planting activities. Through satellite imagery and on-the-ground monitoring, the team tracks the condition and growth of trees over time, ensuring that the right trees are planted in the right places and cared for appropriately.

Moreover, Dr. Goodall emphasizes the importance of technology, both high-tech and low-tech, in addressing environmental challenges. While satellite monitoring and mobile apps facilitate forest restoration efforts, Dr. Goodall recognizes the value of traditional ecological knowledge and low-tech solutions in conservation practices.

Ultimately, Dr. Goodall sees technology as a source of hope in the fight against climate change and biodiversity loss. By leveraging innovative approaches and engaging communities, she believes that we can create a sustainable future for both people and the planet.

In addition to her work with Ecosia, Dr. Goodall has been actively involved in raising awareness about climate change and environmental conservation through initiatives such as the International Women's Earth and Climate Summit. She emphasizes the importance of empowering women and communities to take action and advocates for a shift towards sustainable, nature-friendly practices.

Through her tireless efforts and collaborations with organizations like Ecosia, Dr. Jane Goodall continues to inspire positive change and pave the way for a more sustainable future.

Chapter 7: Enduring Legacy

Dr. Jane Goodall's advocacy efforts transcended geographical boundaries, as she tirelessly worked to raise awareness about conservation and environmental issues on a global scale. Through her lectures, books, documentaries, and public appearances, she reached millions of individuals, inspiring them to take action for the planet. Dr. Goodall transformed the way people perceived their relationship with nature, emphasizing that humans are not separate from the environment but an integral part of it.

One of the lasting legacies of Dr. Goodall's environmental advocacy is the Roots & Shoots program, an initiative of the Jane Goodall Institute (JGI). This program empowers young people worldwide to become compassionate leaders and agents of change in their communities. By nurturing the next generation of conservationists and instilling values of compassion and environmental stewardship, Dr. Goodall's legacy continues to shape the future of conservation efforts.

Despite her advancing age, Dr. Goodall shows no signs of slowing down. As she celebrated her 90th birthday, she remained committed to her demanding schedule of traveling and public speaking engagements. Her enduring passion for conservation and her unwavering dedication to the cause serve as an inspiration to people of all ages.

Dr. Goodall's impact on individuals is profound, as evidenced by the overwhelming admiration and respect she receives wherever she goes. Whether speaking to older generations who remember her as a pioneering scientist or to younger activists who see her as a symbol of wisdom and inspiration, Dr. Goodall's message resonates deeply with people from all walks of life.

At a recent event in Seattle, Dr. Goodall captivated the audience with her stories and insights. Despite her iconic status, she remains humble and grounded, connecting with attendees on a personal level. Her simple yet profound message about hope, tenacity, and our collective responsibility to protect the planet leaves a lasting impression on all who hear her speak.

As Dr. Goodall continues her journey, she remains focused on the urgent need to address climate change, biodiversity loss, and other pressing environmental challenges. Her message of empowerment, empathy, and hope serves as a beacon of light in an increasingly uncertain world. Dr. Jane Goodall's remarkable life and work remind us of the power of individual action and the importance of preserving our planet for future generations.

Testimonials from influenced individuals

The testimonials from individuals who have been influenced by Dr. Jane Goodall's work illustrate the profound impact she has had as a scientist, educator, and advocate for conservation. From her groundbreaking research in Gombe National Park to her role as a mentor and inspiration to countless individuals, Dr. Goodall's legacy is one of passion, empathy, and unwavering dedication to making the world a better place.

Anne Pusey, who worked closely with Dr. Goodall, as a research assistant, highlights her remarkable qualities as a scientist and mentor. Goodall's meticulous observation skills, patience, and sensitivity to the behavior of chimpanzees served as invaluable lessons for Pusey and others who followed in her footsteps. Pusey's experience at Gombe laid the foundation for her own career in evolutionary anthropology, demonstrating the lasting impact of Dr. Goodall's teachings.

Smita Dharsi, an educator, emphasizes Dr. Goodall's role as a teacher and advocate for children. Through her work with the Roots & Shoots program, Dr. Goodall has empowered young people to become compassionate leaders and agents of change in their communities. Dharsi's testimony speaks to the transformative power of Dr. Goodall's educational initiatives and her ability to instill values of empathy, environmental stewardship, and hope in future generations.

Japhet Jonas Mwanangombe, a coordinator for Roots & Shoots in Tanzania, reflects on Dr. Goodall's inspirational leadership and the impact of her teachings on local communities. Dr. Goodall's passion, energy, and empowerment have motivated countless individuals to take action and make a positive difference in the world. Mwanang'ombe's testimony highlights the ripple effect of Dr. Goodall's work, as her teachings continue to inspire change at the grassroots level.

The phenomenon known as "the Jane effect" underscores the profound emotional connection that people feel when encountering Dr. Goodall's message of hope and compassion. As one attendee noted, hearing Dr. Goodall speak filled them with a sense of hope and inspiration, highlighting the transformative power of her words and presence.

Dr. Goodall's ability to view each individual as unique and valuable reflects her inclusive and compassionate approach to advocacy.

As she continues her work, she remains committed to empowering others to join her in collective action to address pressing environmental challenges. Dr. Goodall's vision for a better world emphasizes the importance of collaboration and unity in creating positive change for future generations.

Overall, Dr. Jane Goodall's enduring legacy serves as a beacon of hope and inspiration for individuals around the world. Her teachings and advocacy continue to resonate with people of all ages, fostering a sense of collective responsibility and empowerment in the face of global challenges.

www.ingramcontent.com/pod-product-compliance
Lightning Source LLC
Chambersburg PA
CBHW071217260726

48653CB00041B/891